# Fanciful Dogs in Secret Places

## A DOG LOVER'S COLORING BOOK

Illustrations by
Honoel

Waves of Color

Fanciful Dogs in Secret Places: A Dog Lover's Coloring Book
© 2018 Seven Seas Entertainment, LLC.
All rights reserved.

Artwork by Honoel A. Ibardolaza
Art Assistants: Mariz Eloisa Hechanova, Jehram Dave Jara, & Femy Marie Remilla
Cover Coloring: Ma. Victoria Robado
Logo Design: Courtney Williams
Cover Design: Nicky Lim
Production Manager: Lissa Pattillo
Editor-in-Chief: Adam Arnold
Publisher: Jason DeAngelis

Waves of Color books may be purchased in bulk for promotional, educational, or business use. Please contact your local bookseller or the Macmillan Corporate and Premium Sales Department at 1-800-221-7945, extension 5442, or by e-mail at MacmillanSpecialMarkets@macmillan.com.

Waves of Color and the Waves of Color logo are trademarks of Seven Seas Entertainment, LLC. All rights reserved.

ISBN: 978-1-626927-78-0
Printed in Canada

First Printing: April 2018

10 9 8 7 6 5 4 3 2 1

**Fanciful Dogs in Secret Places**
**A DOG LOVER'S COLORING BOOK**

Illustration Index

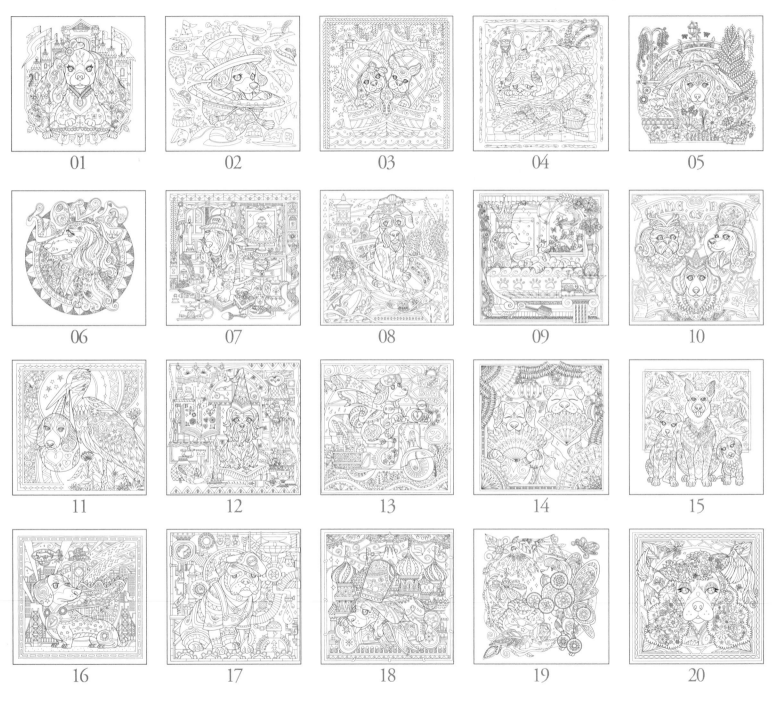

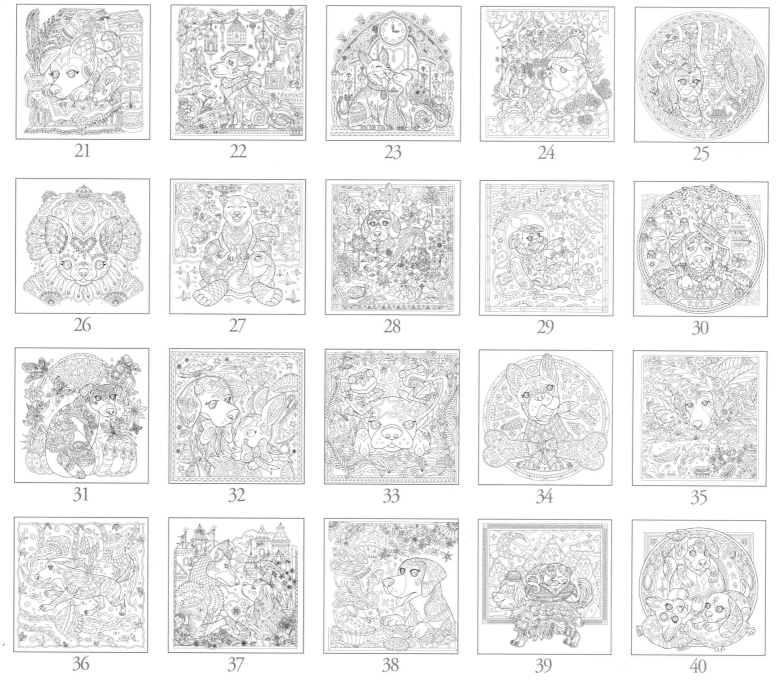

21     22     23     24     25

26     27     28     29     30

31     32     33     34     35

36     37     38     39     40

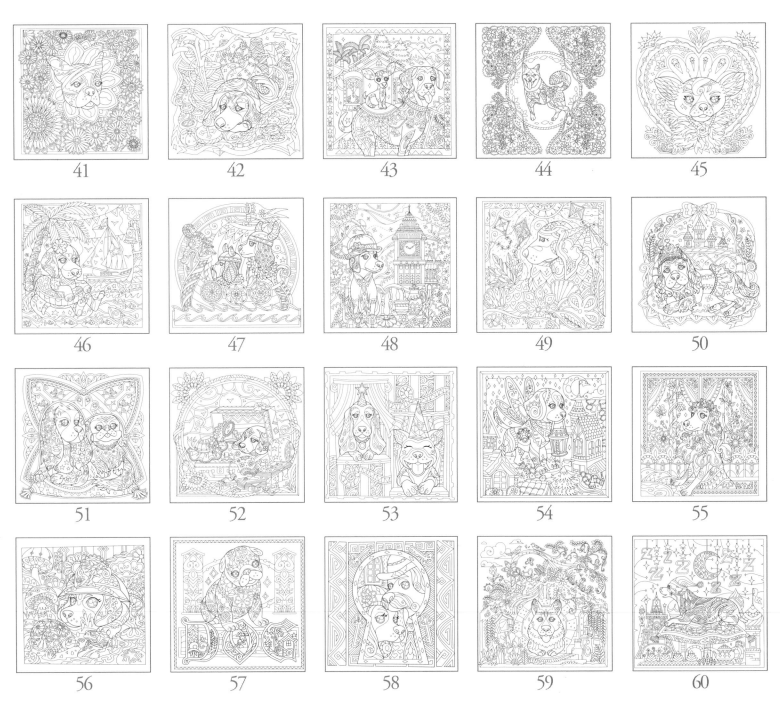

41      42      43      44      45

46      47      48      49      50

51      52      53      54      55

56      57      58      59      60

61

62

63

64

65

66

67

68

69

70

71

72

73

74

75

76

77

78

79

80